Ca

Stephanie King

Illustrated by Claire Vessey

Scripture Union

Copyright © Stephanie King 2002

First published 2002

Scripture Union, 207 - 209 Queensway, Bletchley, Milton Keynes, MK2 2EB, England.

Email: info@scriptureunion.org.uk

Web site: www.scriptureunion.org.uk

ISBN 1 85999 542 X

British Library Cataloguing-in-Publication Data.

A catalogue record of this book is available from the British Library.

Printed and bound in Great Britain by Ebenezer Baylis and Son Ltd., The Trinity Press, Worcester.

Scripture Union is an international Christian charity working with churches in more than 130 countries, providing resources to bring the good news about Jesus Christ to children, young people and families and to encourage them to develop spiritually through the Bible and prayer. As well as our network of volunteers, staff and associates who run holidays, church-based events and school Christian groups, we produce a wide range of publications and support those who use our resources through training programmes.

I like talking to my dad.
We chat while we do things together.

"Do you know," says Dad, "that you can chat to Jesus just like you chat to me?"

"How does Jesus hear me?" I ask.
"Can I phone him? Or use your mobile?

Or e-mail him?"

"You don't need anything at all,"
laughs Dad. "Just talk to him!"

"Can I whisper?
Or do I have to SHOUT?"

"Jesus can hear the tiniest whisper,"
says Dad.

"Even on a mountain?

Or in a submarine?"

"Yes," says Dad. "Jesus is always next to you, and he can hear you anywhere."

"When Jesus lived on earth, he loved children to come and talk to him. He always had time for them."

"Jesus still has time for children. He loves YOU, and he loves to hear you talk to him, any time."

"You can say 'thank you' for all the lovely things that happen to you.

Jesus loves to hear you say thank you!"

"You can say 'help!' when you're in trouble. Jesus really will help you!"

"You can say 'sorry' when you've done something wrong.

Jesus really will forgive you!"

"You can say 'please look after me' when you feel scared.

Jesus really will take care of you!"

"You can say 'Please look after my friends' when they are sad or hurt.

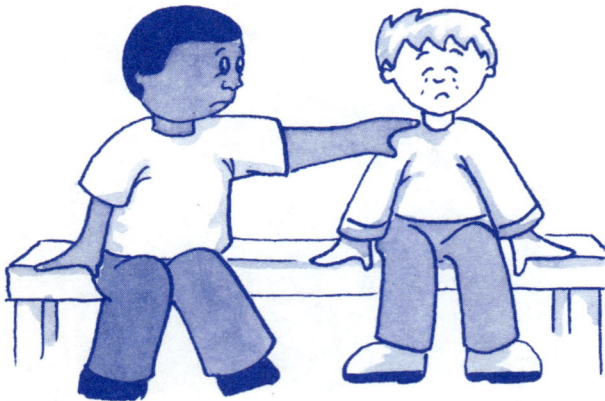

Jesus really will take care of them!"

"And the best bit is," says Dad, "the more you chat to Jesus, the better you get to know him!"

"Can I talk to Jesus now?" I ask Dad.

"Of course," he says,
"any time, anywhere!"

"Thank you, Jesus,
for listening to me."

"Thank you, Jesus, that you love me and look after me."

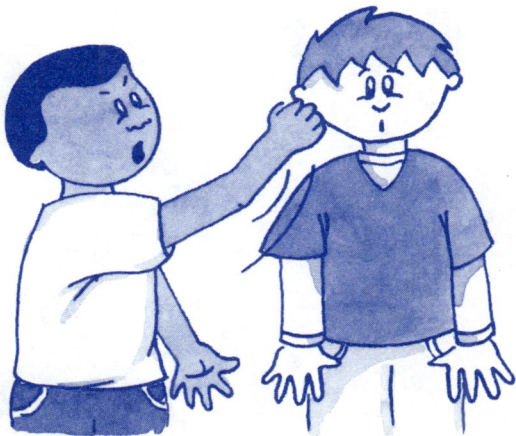

"I'm sorry, Jesus, that I was naughty."

"Please, Jesus, take care of us."

"Please, Jesus, take care of me when I'm at school."

"And thank you, Jesus, that you are always my friend!"